*The following photos are royalty free images from Fotolia.com
Verse 2: Octopus © Richard Carey – Fotolia.com
Verse 5: Snow Angel © Murat Subatli – Fotolia.com
Verse 13: Road to Sun © Pavel Klimenko – Fotolia.com
*The photo accompanying Verse 11: Stormy Water, is a public domain photo from Public-Domain-Photos.com by Paolo Neo.
The vectors used for the star and flares are from VectorLady.com. Comic-SCF font was used for the text of the book.
Disclaimer: Fotolia.com, its photographers, VectorLady.com, and Public-Domain-Images.com do not endorse this book in any way.

Images in this book are a combination of photographs (some of which were edited with HDR imaging, to remove litter, and to accommodate size requirements), computer generated illustrations, and vectors. Comic-SCF font was used for the verses.

KNOWING

All inquiries regarding permission to redistribute parts of this book should be addressed to:
Knowing Publications
P.O. Box 3947
Mansfield, OH 44907
www.loveyourlightbooks.com

First Edition

Printed by CreateSpace

ISBN-13: 978-0615678818
ISBN-10: 0615678815
Title ID. 3954280

Editors: Cinde Carr, Ryan Metz, & Mark Roseberry

LOVE YOUR LIGHT

Written By Julie McPeek

Illustrations by Tim Hull

Photos by Brian McPeek*

*Except where noted

Dedication:
This book is dedicated to my wonderful son, Micah. You are my inspiration and my greatest teacher! You have taught me so much about the beauty of unconditional love. May you lead an amazing life that is full of love, joy, wonder, and adventure!

Acknowledgements:
First and foremost, thank You, God. This book would not be possible without You! I am so blessed, and so grateful!

Thank you to Cinde Carr, Collier Landry, Ryan Metz, Cheryl Pete, and Mark Roseberry. Your time, consideration, and input have helped this little book to grow tremendously. I appreciate you all so much.

Last, but definitely not least, thank you to my wonderful husband, Mike. Your love, patience, care, and insight have helped me more than you know. Thank you for being such a wonderful man.

~1~

There is a light that shines in you

That is loving, pure, and strong,

And it will always help you

To know what's right and wrong.

This light will act to guide your path

And brighten the darkest night!

Always honor who you are

And **ALWAYS LOVE YOUR LIGHT!**

~2~

Your light contains the spark of love

That we each hold within

No matter what you look like—

Any color, large or thin!

Each person deserves this love—

We must keep that in sight!

Always honor who you are

And **ALWAYS LOVE YOUR LIGHT!**

~3~

This light comes from deep inside

And helps us love and grow.

We learn more from it each day

Than we could ever know.

Always keep this fact in mind—

You will climb to such great height!

Always honor who you are

And **ALWAYS LOVE YOUR LIGHT!**

~4~

Sometimes people who've been hurt

May hurt you just for fun,

Like call names and tell untruths

That will make you want to run.

Just know that you deserve love—

You will rise above this plight!

Always honor who you are

And **ALWAYS LOVE YOUR LIGHT!**

~5~

No two people are the same,

Just like unique snowflakes,

And each person has great worth,

Although they've made mistakes.

Forgiveness is essential—

Please heed this great insight!

Always honor who you are

And **ALWAYS LOVE YOUR LIGHT!**

~6~

When you feel hurt or angry,

Spend some time inside their shoes.

Your words may truly hurt them

And leave them with the blues.

Please express yourself in ways

That show thought and do not fight!

Always honor who you are

And **ALWAYS LOVE YOUR LIGHT!**

~7~

Sometimes it will seem easy

To just go with the crowd,

Even when it's wrong or rude—

These acts won't make you proud!

Let all your actions spring from love

And forever be forthright!

Always honor who you are

And **ALWAYS LOVE YOUR LIGHT!**

~8~

Decide to make good choices!

Decide to act from love!

If someone's having a bad day

Give them a big, huge hug!

Your mindset makes a difference—

And that difference is not slight!

Always honor who you are

And **ALWAYS LOVE YOUR LIGHT!**

~9~

It's crucial that you be your best—

Whatever that may be.

Your actions will inspire;

Just listen—you will see!

Have the courage to unleash it

And you will shine so bright!

Always honor who you are

And **ALWAYS LOVE YOUR LIGHT!**

~10~

We all have something inside

So special and unique:

Work daily with these gifts—

Watch your talents reach their peak!

When you're feeling insecure,

Or feeling full of fright,

Always honor who you are

And **ALWAYS LOVE YOUR LIGHT!**

~11~

Stand firmly in your power

And stand firm to your own truth.

Kindness is its own reward—

Of this there's ample proof!

Be courageous, brave, and strong—

Great adventures you'll invite!

Always honor who you are

And **ALWAYS LOVE YOUR LIGHT!**

~12~

You're the one and only you,

So no matter what you do,

If your actions spring from love

You'll shine—please know this truth!

You have beauty deep inside

That is waiting to take flight!

Always honor who you are

And **<u>ALWAYS LOVE YOUR LIGHT!</u>**

~13~

Some day when you are older,
With all these lessons learned,

You'll share this truth with others
Through how your life has turned.

Loving actions change the world—

Even when the acts seem slight.

Always honor who you are

And **ALWAYS LOVE YOUR LIGHT!**